I Am a Good Neighbor

By Maria Nelson

Gareth Stevens
Publishing

Please visit our website, www.garethstevens.com. For a free color catalog of all our high-quality books, call toll free 1-800-542-2595 or fax 1-877-542-2596.

Library of Congress Cataloging-in-Publication Data

Nelson, Maria.
I am a good neighbor / by Maria Nelson.
  p. cm. — (Kids of character)
Includes index.
ISBN 978-1-4339-9022-9 (pbk.)
ISBN 978-1-4339-9023-6 (6-pack)
ISBN 978-1-4339-9021-2 (library binding)
1. Neighborhoods—Juvenile literature. 2. Communities—Juvenile literature. I. Nelson, Maria. II. Title.
HM756.N45 2014
307.33—dc23

Published in 2014 by
Gareth Stevens Publishing
111 East 14th Street, Suite 349
New York, NY 10003

Designer: Nicholas Domiano
Editor: Kristen Rajczak

Photo credits: Cover, pp. 1 © iStockphoto.com/YinYang; pp. 5, 13 Stockbyte/Thinkstock.com; p. 7 BananaStock/Thinkstock.com; p. 9 Image Source/the Agency Collection/Getty Images; p. 11 Nina Shannon/E+/Getty Images; pp. 17, 21 iStockPhoto/Thinkstock.com; p. 15 Brand X Pictures/Thinkstock.com; p. 19 Blend Images/Shutterstock.com.

Printed in the United States of America

CPSIA compliance information: Batch #CS13GS: For further information contact Gareth Stevens, New York, New York at 1-800-542-2595.

Contents

Boldface words appear in the glossary.

What's a Good Neighbor?

The word "neighbor" often means the people who live in the houses near us. But anyone you meet can be your neighbor, too! Good neighbors are friendly and **considerate** of others. They're helpful, too.

Paul and his family had just moved to a new neighborhood. He didn't know anyone there. A group of kids riding bikes stopped to say hello. They were friendly and welcoming. They were being good neighbors.

TaNisha's next-door neighbors went on vacation. They asked her for help while they were gone. Every day, TaNisha fed their cat and watered their plants. TaNisha was a good neighbor because she was so helpful.

Return to Sender

When Diane checked her family's mailbox, she saw they got a letter for her neighbor. It was **delivered** to the wrong address! Diane walked down the street and gave her neighbor the letter. She was a good neighbor.

Clean Up!

On a windy day, Louis saw some trash blow into the street. He got a bag, collected the trash, and put it back in the garbage can. By helping keep his street clean, Louis was being a good neighbor.

Aman offered to **mow** his neighbor's lawn. Mr. Bennett had hurt his back and couldn't do it himself. Aman was a good neighbor. He helped someone who was hurt and made the neighborhood look nice!

15

Don't Wake the Baby

Kayleen was having a pool party! She and her friends were splashing and jumping. When it got dark, Kayleen asked them to come inside. Her next-door neighbor had a baby who needed quiet to sleep. Kayleen was a good neighbor.

A Helping Hand

Devon saw his neighbor having trouble with her grocery bags. Devon ran over to help her carry them. Good neighbors help each other when needed. Devon was a good neighbor.

Pierre wanted to do something nice for his neighbor. She was very sick. He and his dad made dinner to take to her family. Pierre showed how to be a good neighbor. He was kind and **compassionate**.

Glossary

compassionate: showing a wish to help someone who is having a hard time

considerate: thoughtful of the feelings of others

deliver: to take and hand over

mow: to cut grass

For More Information

Books

Lyons, Shelly. *People in My Neighborhood.* North Mankato, MN: Capstone Press, 2013.

Owens, L. L. *Meet Your Neighborhood.* Edina, MN: Magic Wagon, 2011.

Websites

Build a Neighborhood
pbskids.org/rogers/buildANeighborhood.html
Build your own neighborhood to help you think of ways to be a good neighbor.

Zoom into Action: You Can Help in Your Neighborhood!
pbskids.org/zoom/activities/action/way08.html
Use this website to find out ways you can be a good neighbor.

Index